What people are

Lost for

A wonderful homage to beauty, silence and joy. The words are here only as a pretext to express the purity of the being. They dress the silence, give it a form, and dissolve into their origin. No trace remains. Thank you!
Dr Jean-Marc Mantel, psychiatrist, non-dual teacher, author of *The Scent of Oneness*

An extraordinary (and unexpected) outpouring of poems from within the Covid lockdown. How strange that constriction opens into space!
Nigel Wellings, psychoanalytic psychotherapist, author of *Why can't I meditate?*

This collection of poems plunges us into the reality that lies behind our everyday thoughts, experiences, and imaginings. Martin uses fable, parable, the facts of living and dying, the great questions we ask ourselves, his own experiences and those of family and friends, to reveal to himself and to us the essential unity of our existence on this earth. His verse, with its natural cadences and vivid and simple images, points us gently to an authentic understanding of why we are here and invites us at every turn to live a deeper truth available to us all.
Vaughn Malcolm, linguist, musician, long time meditator and student of non-duality

Reading this beautiful collection of poems created within me an invitation to an experience of dropping, gently and deeply, into the wisdom of the non-dual path. Through these poems, Martin encourages and accompanies us into the simplicity and spaciousness of living from a sense of belonging and identity beyond our familiar, constructed sense of self. His poems call for tenderness towards the pain of our constricted living and the ways in which we can imprison ourselves and others. Each poem is a call from the deep – to reimagine and to reconnect with ourselves from the perspective of infinite compassion, and to live into the freedom (and responsibility) of our belonging. Within and between these words is an insistent call to 'wake up' to the inherent preciousness of our being, beyond anything that we can 'do'. Martin's poems are a gift and an inspiration to live lightly and courageously within this precious freedom.

Dr Claire Davis, NHS Consultant psychotherapist

Lost for Words

The poetry of mindfulness
and non-duality

Lost for Words

The poetry of mindfulness
and non-duality

Martin Wells

MANTRA
BOOKS

Winchester, UK
Washington, USA

JOHN HUNT PUBLISHING

First published by Mantra Books, 2022
Mantra Books is an imprint of John Hunt Publishing Ltd., No. 3 East Street, Alresford
Hampshire SO24 9EE, UK
office@jhpbooks.com
www.johnhuntpublishing.com
www.mantra-books.net

For distributor details and how to order please visit the 'Ordering' section on our website.

ISBN: 978 1 78535 931 6
978 1 78535 932 3 (ebook)
Library of Congress Control Number: 2021950036

A CIP catalogue record for this book is available from the British Library.

Design: Matthew Greenfield

UK: Printed and bound by CPI Group (UK) Ltd, Croydon, CR0 4YY
Printed in North America by CPI GPS partners

We operate a distinctive and ethical publishing philosophy in
all areas of our business, from our global network of authors to
production and worldwide distribution.

Contents

Also by the Author

Sitting in the Stillness
Mantra books, John Hunt Publishing, 2020
ISBN 978-1-78904-266-5

No one Playing
Mantra books, John Hunt Publishing, 2022
ISBN 978-1-78904-781-3

Acknowledgements

My heartfelt thanks to Sue, my wife, for the inspiration, the encouragement – for showing me the value of risking a step out of the ordinary into the unknown.

Also, many thanks to Vaughn and Charlie for the wonderful and supportive editing.

To Jean-Marc Mantel for the life-changing introduction to our true nature – to the creative presence beyond ego.

To my Kiwi buddy Mark Davis who died in the period these poems arrived and whose love of poetry was part of the inspiration for this collection. A poem he wrote a few weeks before he died is an appendix to this book.

To my dear NHS colleagues for their encouragement.

To those great poets, Rumi, Eliot, Oliver, Gibran and many more who have pointed to the eternal joy of this life in the ordinary and even in the painful.

To John Hunt Publishing for taking the risk with a book of poems from an unknown poet.

Prologue

Between midnight and dawn, when the past is all deception,
The future futureless, before the morning watch
When time stops and time is never ending.... T.S.Eliot*

In the early hours of almost every morning during the Covid lockdown in the months of March and April 2021, these poems began mysteriously arriving – like persistent early morning visitors. Curiously, my wife was absent for the whole of this time and, much to her amusement, in her place lay an open notebook, a blank page and a pen. Soon nearly forty poems filled the notebook – I had never written poetry in my life before.

Each poem was stirred into being by what was going on at the time. Every human being was affected by the global pandemic and faced with fears of illness, death and isolation. The cracks we had been papering over became exposed, including racism, domestic violence, greed and inequality, climate change. The worst about us highlighted but also the best: the courage and sacrifice of frontline workers, the power of community, inspirational people raising huge sums for charity. We were reminded of the simple things that matter: of family, of music and of the natural world.

Although the pandemic provides the foreground for these poems, they have also been prompted by timeless universal themes, symbolised in a snowdrop or an olive tree, in conversations about love and life and death, in news items and random images. But, most of all, they have risen out of that deep longing for union and freedom at the source of each of us.

As you read this collection of poems, I hope you may feel like a fellow traveller on the road back home to yourself.

* T.S. Eliot, 1943, *The Four Quartets*, Faber and Faber, London.

The Responsibilities of a Snowdrop

I must wait patiently in the cold, dark earth,
until the call of the light.
When the call comes, I must remember to leave half of my
being
in the darkness,
thankfully.
And when the call comes, I must be ready,
but not push too hard,
simply allow myself to be drawn up,
and to remember there is no me,
just merging emerging,
playing its small part in one being.

And in the light, I must be brave.
The brightness will be excruciating,
the air joyously exposing,
the freedom terrifying.
I must remember the earth in which I stand;
only then
is my true nature free.

And in the air will be birds and insects
and massive beings.
I must remember to give this body
joyously
to whatever is its fate.
And remember my source is eternal.

And I need not compare myself
to similar of my kind;
just stand in my allotted place –

not proudly,
but secure in recalling
the source which allows
this simple wondrous being.

Lost for Words

Shall we live in a land of verbs?
Could we see more clearly?
Life seeing itself.
Just seeing.
Subject and object no more.
The end of 'it' and 'you' and 'me',
no one there,
just living, loving.

Could we dare to lose
the deadened, static noun?
The great separator,
the killjoy
who pins the butterfly to the board –
lifeless.
We might then see the space in which it flies,
the light in its wings
alighting.
Really see the petal on which it's sitting
and the dewdrop
clinging,
and all in the breeze
dancing.
And for all this,
thanking.

We say: 'I took a breath in,
and I breathe out.'
No! there is only breathing,
no 'I', no 'in', no 'out',
no thing called 'breath'.

Only breathing,
happening.

We say: 'I don't belong in this place',
like a wave saying it does not belong
in the ocean.
In the land of verbs there is only
belonging.

And in the land of no nouns
would we see things as they really are?
The hard edges dissolved,
no separation.
No one writing this
and to no one else.
Just life resonating.
Say, 'I wrote you a poem' and
the poem is dead.

But how hard to lose my nouns.
Perhaps only in silence
can it all be said.

The Ant and the Ostrich

Part I

Why do you hide your head in this sand
and leave the rest of your body out there?
You cannot even see me,
so I'll whisper in your ear.

I fear for your survival.
You hide your head
and run like the wind
but have forgotten how to fly.

Are you a bird?
Other birds weave patterns in the sky
of their togetherness.

Brother, I fear for you and those like you
and say this out of friendship.
My clan is so tiny,
we had to learn to work together.
To pursue our own needs would have been fatal.

We have learnt to carry our burdens together
with joy
and no thought for the individual load.
How amazing what can be carried by each one
when the weight is shared.
If I thought about how heavy my personal suffering was
I would collapse.
We face the task ahead as One.
My brothers and sisters will survive

long after the individual forms are gone.

Please lift your head up
and face what's there.
Seek out brothers and sisters –
you might not make it alone.

Your beautiful original form
might not continue to grace this land,
walking tall
under our vast blue sky.

Part II

The Ostrich lifts his head out of the sand,
laughing.
Thank you for your concern my brother,
but I'm not hiding,
this is our survival.

Ha! The assumptions we make
about our differences –
all in the mind.

If I didn't turn these eggs, hidden in the sand,
to keep them warm
they would not live,
and like you if I only
thought of me,
then life could not go on.

I must ignore the danger
in the not seeing.
And yet even in the darkness,

you reach out in friendship and love
and in the service
of us all.

Ending It All

No shame in the wish to end it all
but also no need to destroy the body.
No need for self-harm.
Simply follow this wish back to its source
and put your ear to the ground
of your being
and listen.

Peace and freedom are calling
and not from afar.
How could you know them
unless they are what you are?
I could <u>tell</u> you about the ice-cold surf against skin,
describe the smell of seaweed
and the crackle of the pebbles
as the waves draw back
but still you would not know it.

We only know freedom because
we are that.
The source of being.
So 'yes' to ending it all.
End the illusion.
End the story of you.
Say goodbye to the self,
consumed by thought and belief.

End the search for repair;
there's nothing to fix.
There is pain in this living
but you are not to blame.

End the 'me' thoughts that shame.
End all that is not truly you
and come home to the being
before all thought,
so perfect and peaceful and free.

If You Choose Comfort

If you choose comfort,
smooth out the pain,
what will you have learnt?

If you take the bypass,
speeding past the world,
what will you have seen?

If you only swim on the surface,
never sink to the ocean floor,
how will you know depth?
How will you know your capacity
to return from darkness?

If you've never spent time confined,
how will you know the sweet taste of freedom?

If you never feel completely alone,
how will you know connection?
If you have not felt being on the outside,
how will you know belonging?

If you have not looked death in the face,
how will you know life?
Will you have really seen the blossom,
truly heard the birdsong?

If you have never been hungry,
how can you value the crumbs?
If you choose a world of plenty,
will you know the value of small things?

If you choose ego over service,
will you ever know why you're here?
If you never choose surrender
over winning,
will you ever know humility and grace?

But choose silence and solitude
and you might hear
love's music
and in true emptiness,
might know the fullness
of your heart.

'A Hidden Life'

Here lies Jane Smith.
You won't have heard of her.
She gave life through sacrifice,
made mistakes,
but in every moment did her best.

She was never on TV,
her little flat was not her own.
She really tried to make her marriage work,
to make the most of what she had,
but the bruising would not stop.

So she took the hero's journey,
out into the unknown
with her flock.
Penniless but free,
safer but not safe,
facing other new fears
with enough courage
to inspire a thousand lives.

Nothing shiny or exciting
but an ordinary love
expressed.
A life given so that others could be free
fulfilling Nature's perfect plan.

A Hundred Days in Lockdown

Will I thump against the door hoping to be let out?
Will I find a thousand things for the boredom?
Will I pace up and down until it's time?
Will all the parcels give life meaning?

Perhaps the culprit will come forward
so I can join the other judges.

Or maybe like a prisoner
at peace with his fate,
I can learn to love the light
that illuminates this cell.
Let all the wanting fall away
into delicious freedom,
take that path from loneliness
to solitude.
Perhaps that emptiness can be enjoyed?
Such an unfamiliar space.

Perhaps the silence that was so hard to bear
becomes an everlasting friend?
And when that day comes
when we are unlocked,
I might truly smell the first rose
along my path.

No Birth Without Contraction

No birth comes without contraction.
These big steps we take in life
are rarely smooth
nor should they be.

We need to feel the depth of our clinging
to what has served us so well,
to honour today's problem
that was yesterday's solution.
And don't berate the stuckness,
celebrate the creativity.

We are being born and have no choice,
the change already here
and started long ago.
Only welcome all it brings.
What's being born in us can thrive
and what's been before
can dissolve in our respectful gaze.

Let Love attend the birth
so all parts are one,
as is Nature's way.

A Birth continued...

And out in the world of light and space
a new freedom,
no longer held in safety,
old structures gone.

The freedom we seek
offers no containment,
no surrounding walls,
the end of the familiar
and what was always known.

Nothing to cling to
as we're drawn out into spacious being.
A fledgling comes of age
to know itself,
as in and of the vast
blue sky of freedom.

As I Awake

As I awake from a dream
I ask, what is real?
The dream seemed real
but so does life.
I was running in fear,
shallow breath,
dry mouth,
heart beating.

But then by day there's fear
and forms of running
from imaginary danger.
I might be seen for who I am,
disguise and mask no use.
And then far worse,
there comes the axe
of membership withdrawn,
pushed out from the tribe
in shame and vulnerability.

Is this too a dream?
Same pulse racing.
Is this the old, old story,
the childhood nightmare?

Within the dream
I need to strive,
body tense and sweating.
I need to play the role so well
and all the time forgetting.

So what it is to finally awake,
life's dream exposed.
The running stops,
the body's tensions fall away,
the mirage now revealed.

How clear the air is now,
how still the body.
The mind still rattles on and on
but now seen for what it is:
weaver of dreams,
teller of stories,
the great imposter.
What is awake is not the mind,
not thought or deeply held belief
but simple silent witnessing
and delicious clarity.
Just space is left
and what was me dissolves.
What seemed to be real
just seen as story.

Should I look back with regret?
Was I a fool to sleep so long?
Or is that just the way it is?
It seems to make the waking up so sweet,
like walking from the city's noise and smog
into the fresh, clear mountain air.
But in the next invite to sleep,
will I remember?

On Knowing How to Live and Love
(dedicated to Mark – who does)

'What's this queue for?'
'This is where we give these costumes
back to the earth.'
'What do you mean?'
'Some call it death.'

'But I'm not ready.'
'It doesn't work like that.'

'There's so many things
left unsaid,
so many fights
unnecessarily fought,
so many empty victories.

So many shiny things
that promised much,
but now just reflect
this ageing face.

How many roses have I passed,
unnoticed?
How many words of love were missed
with too much in the diary?

I never got to see the starlings;
too many thrillers on TV.

There were friends and much to say
but not of any depth.

Never what they meant to me
or how I held them in my heart.'

'But that's the reason for the queue,
a chance to stand and wait,
be still and contemplate
the inner regions of the heart.

And what remains,
when body turns to dust.'

'What does remain?'

'Don't confuse this body
with your being,
it's simply clothing.
Without it what's left
is not the thing called "me",
but the space in which you've lived,
infinite and free.'

The Park Bench

What joy to bear the weight of friendship,
the patter of the toddler's feet,
the solitary lunch consumed,
to stand here in the stillness
with such a simple task.

To hear the stories light and dark,
to bear it all
with equanimity.
Mine not to judge
or take one side
against another.

And not see the good or bad
but simply hold it lightly
with all my being,
a role so clear and simple.
I play my part as others do,
rooted in the earth
and holding up the sky.
Each movement of the tree is mine,
each bird my freedom,
the joy of standing quiet
and knowing what I am.

Lecture Given to the Royal College of Psychiatrists: Dr Jean-Marc Mantel

He had no notes,
no PowerPoint,
no facts and figures to report,
no research to prove his case,
no clinical examples.

There's far more space than words it seems
as though the space is what he's teaching.
Each phrase has silence
as a friend
as though reminding,
words ringing like a bell
into the emptiness.

There seemed no attempt to teach
and yet the teaching was profound,
no progress to be made,
just what was here and now,
no path to take,
just this sweet moment.

Nothing complicated,
no knowledge needed,
just this and only this.
No actions recommended,
no skills to practise,
nothing to be grasped,
no things at all.
Instead a simple invitation
to live the truth of what we are,

to be the love when 'I' is not.

Surrender to the silence.
Be less concerned with all the doing
and open to our being.
Stop the endless searching
and come home to what we are:
the source and essence of the self.
Remember all that came before
and the limits of our stories.

He pointed to that freedom,
right there, right then,
and the stillness of our being.
No need for audience or followers,
no programme to be joined,
but here a deep release,
a stillness so profound,
a joining in the silence,
and simple gratitude.

The Roots of Love

The roots of love cannot be seen
but only surely known;
every year growing deeper,
yes, in the darkness
but married to the light
as perfect mirrors,
two aspects of the One.

The joyous gifts of leaf and flower
not possible without the depth;
the reaching for the sky
by earth supported,
earth nourished in the reaching.
Nature's balanced being
a mirror to the human eye
if only it will open.

Each human love reflected
in the dewdrop on the rose
and every distant star –
life on Earth's reminders
of what we truly are.

The Pugilist

Why hold your fists so tightly?
The danger's in the past.
The tension needed then –
it kept you from more harm,
the little sentry at the gate,
no one coming through,
a hardened heart
and calloused hand.

The fists so fixed in one position,
so cramped in this one mode,
they can't know tenderness,
can't know who's friend
and who is foe.
The heart so steadfastly protected,
safe but so alone.
Each beat infused with fear
and this must not be shown.

And such a yearning to be free,
to play another part,
allow another in
to the deepest regions of the heart.

Even noticing this rigid pose
a softening occurs,
the early signs of thawing out.
But numbness gone
the pain arises
and shame and vulnerability.
Too late to turn back now,

your traumas are revisited.
But courage so long by your side,
now performs another role,
a different sort of ally.
'Let go,' it says.
'Surrender to what's here,
step into the unknown,
embrace your deepest fear.
Risk opening your heart
and letting others in.
Risk giving up control,
your castle gate already breached,
fresh air replacing stale.
Who knows who saunters in?
What gifts they bring
what forms they take,
opportunities disguised.'

What felt safe back then
now falls apart,
the old illusion crumbles,
a deeper truth revealed,
the safety of surrender.
The heart now open and exposed
beating in another rhythm,
in simple harmony with love,
a symphony of freedom.

The Olive Tree

A thousand years of standing here
have left me old and gnarled.
I've seen many of them come and go,
the ones they call the owners.

And all the stories I could tell
of war and pain and laughter;
the same children that once climbed in me
became lovers at my feet,
and soon after dust that feeds my roots –
and round and round again.

And many came and sat and wondered why,
some close enough to hear my one reply:
Come, come closer,
I'll whisper it to you.

The Caterpillar and the Psychotherapist

Session 1

So glad to hear this space was free;
I'm so worried for myself.
I feel deep change is coming on,
perhaps a midlife crisis?
I fear it all might fall apart,
I'm heading for a breakdown;
there must be something you can do,
some remedy or potion?
'Trust the process' will not do –
I fear it's getting worse.

Session 2

I don't know why I talk to you,
the breakdown's now complete.
All structure's gone – all safety.
I told you this was coming!
'Accept,' you say,
behind that sickly reassuring smile.
With your fine wings and lovely colours,
you can't know what I'm going through.

Session 3

I'm feeling ready to emerge,
if you would only help me.
I just can't do it by myself,
at least give me some advice,
some skills to help me out of here.

Perhaps a surgeon's what I need
to take away this plaster?
'All will be well' is not enough –
you've got to set me free!

Session 4

I came today to say my thanks.
As you can see, I'm free.
I see now why you were so still,
such peaceful understanding;
there was no problem after all,
just the workings of my mind.
No doing needed on your part;
or mine too it seems.
When I'd looked into your eyes,
I'd seen a quiet knowing,
the deepest reassurance
to trust in Nature's loving plan,
to watch and wait
and see the wonder of it all.

The Purpose of a Rose

With nothing in the diary,
two roses stood in silence
until one said:
'People often ask
what is the meaning of all this?'

'That's easy,' replied his neighbour.
'To be the best that I can be.'

'But there's no purpose,'
said his friend.
'You have no choice along the way,
no individual path.
You only have to stop and look
to see we're all connected.'

'That can't be so!'
the other said.
'My job is clear to me:
I rise up from the earth,
hold my head up to the sky
and catch dew drops on my petals.
I'll make a certain fragrance
which calls to other beings.
I freely give them what I have
so they in turn can live.'

'All that is true my friend
apart from one illusion.
There is no *you* who's doing this,
no personal intention.

You're not the author of your fate.
There is a greater power
that brings us all together.
No need for us to question why,
we live to live it seems,
to be the beauty that we are,
not limited in time and space.
An everlasting fragrance.'

Silence Fulfilled

Without the blankness of this page
these words could not exist.
If spoken they'd need silence,
a space in which to be.
A painting needs a canvas,
a dance the background stillness,
but silence needs no words
nor space the world of things.

The background needs no foreground
except to know itself.
The silence is alone fulfilled
and does not need the poet,
although it calls him home
and back into the source.

His words, then, our reminders
of this shared silent presence,
the beings that we are.

Not Separate

You live on the other side of the world
and yet you don't.
You're right here.
You've been told you're dying
and yet you're not,
only your tired body
coming back to the earth.

As the sun sets where you are,
under the long white cloud,
our dawn chorus begins.
Brothers separated
by the whole planet
but not.
Apart in time and space
but only this.

This separation and sorrow,
like the distant church bell,
reminding
of what can never be lost,
the grief in equal measure
to all that has been shared.

Farewell my friend,
but know
that as this great Earth tips forward
we will soon be illuminated
by the light that shone on you –
your night, our day,
the light that seems to change

but never, never goes away.

Man's Best Friend (for Bella and Maisie)

Of all the teachings I've received
yours is the clearest.
It came without conditions,
with such simplicity.

Live each day as new,
no grudges hold.
Don't hesitate or think things through,
run headlong into what comes next.
Treat everyone the same
and every moment of the day
as the best thing that could happen.
Let go of the past
and what you felt
in the midst of some old story.
Be present now!
And even when your friend is gone
their lessons linger on and on.

On Contrast

How strange these prison walls
should speak to me of freedom,
that my shadow
should remind me of the light,
that my loneliness
of sweet solitude,
that all those illusions
should point to what is real,
that division should remind us of the One.

Dear Virus

Dear Virus,
I see that I've learnt most
from the toughest things I've faced,
found freedom when cracked open,
been woken by the loudest noise
and rising after falling.

Now you knock on every door
demanding recognition,
facing every human being
with the greatest challenge
to wake us from a dream,
to break ego's tune,
return to Nature's harmony,
to know there's no real freedom
without responsibility,
to turn from fear to love,
to know the only way to live
is in community.

And no being superior,
no tribe entitled,
no gender in ascendance.
Please wake us up –
we're heading for disaster,
destroying our own home,
our wondrous paradise.
Greed and grasping rule our lives;
in our deep sleep forgetting
the only things that matter.

Dear Human

Dear Human,
You say you'll change
but we shall see.
I'm already changing every day,
no history's binding me.
Look back at your CV,
at all the wars and conflicts,
at your stupidity.

Your leaders strut and pose,
in love with their reflections.
Your children's blood is on their hands.
They kill their own for some idea
or from some deep and tribal fear.

Going back to normal is your wish.
This suits the few but not the many,
the white man in his tailored suit,
bloated with entitlement,
but not the infant in the ghetto;
and not your precious planet
who took a breath while you could not,
its air and water clearing.
In those same months
your stacks of coins fell over,
bank notes blew away,
the biggest debt unpaid.

Go back to normal if you like;
ignore the things I've shown you.
Forget the global village,

head back into your bunker,
protect your shiny things,
dust off the blindfold and the earplugs –
but load your gun. You never know
when the poor come knocking,
the starving distant cousin
going back to normal.

PS A personal note to the military leader of Myanmar.

Dear Min Aung Hlaing,
I saw you with your medals,
saluting tanks and men,
all glinting in the sun.
I watched and watched and wondered
if the latest shiny medal
was for today's brave act:
the enemy a baby,
rubber bullet in his eye.

Wake up you idiot!
That same gold hanging on
your puffed-up chest
adorns your country's temples,
built simply to remember
the teachings of a man
who spoke of love and kindness.
His wisdom lasts for ever,
long after you're just dust.

Carpe Diem

You say 'seize the day'
but of this there is no way.
These things are not for grasping,
the shaft of light,
the bird in flight,
just momentary joys.

No movement of the mind or hand
can ever hold these,
and, if you could,
both hand and mind would close
with no space for what comes next.

So open to the day
with heart and soul and body,
each breath refreshing.
Be like a leaf in the wind
with nothing to hold on to.

Lily's Gift

Can't quite believe you're four today;
this year has gone too fast.
Another year of joy and laughter
but marked by something else.
A whole year of what you call 'the germs',
of standing far apart.
For us no hugs, no bedtime stories,
no morning breakfast fun;
the lovely way you snuggle in
when anything is done;
and most of all the natural wisdom
we grown-ups have forgotten –
a love without conditions,
a reaching out so pure and clear,
arms wide open.

As we go back to normal
I hope I can remember
the sadness and the loss:
sweet reminders
of how love should really be.

By the Sea

The pebbles crackled,
relentless breakers unfolded,
no one swam that day.

But Not Seen

Can we say this happened?
No witness to report it,
only vibrations.

The Stickiness of Ego

I thought I'd let you go,
was mostly free of what you do,
was off the endless see-saw.

But you keep holding on –
or is it me to you?
Does fear creep into my soul
during freedom's emptiness?

Am I like the junkie in withdrawal
knocking at my dealer's door,
seeking bittersweet rewards?
The latest fix might make me whole,
bring personal fulfilment.

If only I can let it go,
surf the strongest impulse,
ride the wave of panic,
abandon all security,
and end all thoughts of me.

Dear India

So many troubled times you've seen,
so much conflict,
so much greed
and massive inequality.

And yet a timeless peace is there
in every fibre of your being.
No words can do this justice
but, if I really listen,
there's just a chance to hear
the silence of your marketplace,
the stillness of your thronging crowd,
the one long note that plays
behind each shop's sitar,
behind each screeching crow
and every chugging tuk tuk.

You're not my home
and yet you are,
quietly reminding
that all things shall pass,
not one thing disturbing
your love and understanding.
All life's agitations dissolving
in the quiet healing warmth
of your all-accepting gaze.

Tres haikus por favor

Winding mountain road,
misty village, white, clinging,
tapas and laughter.

Flamenco singer,
pleading voice of the heart,
gypsies' tears falling.

Hot tarmac, prickly pear,
descafeinado con leche,
smoky talk of old men.

In Gratitude

A heartfelt thanks for all the gifts
that arrive before the dawn,
for all the ink that flows
through this receptive pen,
for all the words that come
to fill my head and heart.
For ease of speech, I say 'they're mine'
but this does not convey
a flow from somewhere else,
half dreams, half passive images.
Yes, water's here,
but flat without a current,
surging, streaming, vibrant.
A seed blown off the static tree,
without a plan or a direction.
Life's seeming random cycle.
Or as each breath unbidden,
not chosen or constructed,
the joy of being breathed.

I am the heart, the vital organ,
pumping energy and blood,
but not the source, the mystery,
not seen but everywhere;
in every trickling brook or crashing wave,
in every field of corn and hungry lion's roar,
in the swooping of the buzzard
and the landing of the snowflake.
River and bank, nectar and bee –
all life's wonders
glimpsed

in precious harmony.

In truth no one to thank;
perhaps just that desert flower's joy
when autumn rains come thumping down,
both rain and flower and saturated earth
forever changed.

We Need Darkness

It's official;
I saw it on the news:
we need darkness.

Vast night sky
reminding,
putting us in our place.
Tiny forms looking up
at the scale of the cosmos
unprotected by our neon bubble.

But the man did not mention this,
the most delicious twist.
Yes, the puny form is what we are
but also every distant star
and all the space surrounding.

True darkness
is the friend
that helps us
look out on ourselves.
How strange the artificial light
that we create
should keep us from reality.

In the Wind

On the line
crisp, white linen sheet
in the wind.
Just this.

Behind, perfectly still,
distant mountain,
in contrast,
standing not waiting,
ancient.

Above, acid blue sky,
boundaryless,
timeless.
Only this.

The eye looks out
but who sees?
Distinct,
not separate.
I am that.
All is one.
Om.

For Sue

You're not who they said you were,
not who they needed you to be,
distorted by their own deep fears.
No blame.

Now a diamond sparkling,
the warmth of the afternoon sun,
lighting up us all.
See how it all returns
in love and heartfelt friendship,
and in your daughter's daughter's eyes,
adoring.

You've freed them both,
a painful story not passed on.
No limits; only inspiration and
the gift of being who you are.

Für Muttichen

The drone of British bombers,
home and town now flat and burning,
young brother missing, never found.
Family fractured, scattered,
refugees.

Faded photo,
English officer and you,
happy, smoking,
bonded for life.

New and strange,
unwelcoming home,
some calling you enemy,
still caught in their conflict.
But only peace and courage
in your young heart,
a heritage remembered
without a burden.
A different sort of battle won,
the victory of peace
and natural equality.
Ich sage vielen dank, Omi.

The Whirling Dervish

As we watch him spin,
faster and faster,
white skirts ballooning,
among all the movement
one word cries out:
Stillness.

A Meditation

Pay less attention
to the world of things and words,
less attention to your thoughts,
less attention to the foreground.
Let this reveal the silence,
the void, the empty space...

...Now be aware of your body again,
Gently recalling the space
and the silent background.
These words need this page,
but the page has no need of words.

From Fiction to Freedom

See how our character moves across the stage
treading familiar steps,
mouthing worn-out lines,
of comfort and familiarity;
how others play their parts
in roles of reciprocity.
A dance prescribed from years before,
decisions made and costumes chosen
in the sponge-like state of infancy.
Family and culture absorbed,
trauma made personal
and into lifelong guiding fiction*
but only ever story,
now viewed from where we sit
in quiet audience.
Life's chronic agitations
all seen from the stillness
of our distant seat,
silently observing
what always seemed like me.

And there's the glimpse of freedom.
The actor may continue on
to strut across the stage,
still holding tightly to the script,
but now no longer me –
a part I sometimes play
for old time's sake
in lazy mediocrity,
in search of what is known,
a compromised security.

But if I dare to leave the stage,
the comfort of the wooden floor
and patterns of addiction,
I step out into the space
of glorious unknowing.
Cold turkey for the ego
but freedom for the soul.

The next scene now an open field,
no map or plan in hand,
next act unwritten.
No lines to follow,
canvas blank and waiting.
A being free to be itself,
each new step as if on mountain snow,
untrodden.

*ref: Alfred Adler

The Thorns of Shame*

How the thorns of shame close around the heart.
Nothing can be said
in years of painful isolation.
Nothing shared
within the ice-cold fear
of exposure.
Any thawing out
a tender pain renewed.
Men in trenches,
heads down,
shivering.
Women voiceless
in passive acquiescence.
Neither stepping into that unknown field
where humiliation
may become humility.

No inner work
heals this wound.
Only in the friendship
of fellow travellers
can the heart dissolve
in the shared warmth of acceptance.
Here the darkest thought,
or memory
melts into the mutual embrace
of each new present moment
and the deepest union of the soul.

*With thanks to my dear colleagues Rob and Tom for our 'meeting' and for the inspiration.

No Ending

Nature has no endings,
no beginnings.
These are for the bookstore
and the mind of man.

In the real world
form simply changes form:
lava to rock, rock to dust,
snow to ice to water,
rose becoming compost,
compost becoming rose.

What's not been born
can never die.

Appendices

My great friend Mark Davis wrote this poem at the end of 2020, a few weeks before he died. It was inspired by some friends lighting a candle to him on their travels in Europe. This poem and his love of poetry planted a seed which bore fruit as Mark was dying.

The Candles of Fatima

In Fatima's sepulchral space
Light and darkness merge in grace.

Tiers of trembling flames stand tall, reach up for life,
And yearn to flourish strong and true.
Each one a soul, of timeless moments, to be and do.

Let us now bless them, and,
Let us now grieve them – deeply,
As if our hearts would break from love.

We bow, and step back, to the door of the day,
We let them go – as they left us.
They flicker with life –
Yet, they too melt and die, into that dark, unknown peace.

Appendices: Web based resources

https://mantel.pro – Dr Jean-Marc Mantel's website with many articles, talks and meditations on non-duality.

https://www.non-dualmindfulness.com – the author's own website with information about retreats, meetings and links to articles and interviews.

About the Author

Martin Wells has worked as a consultant psychotherapist in the NHS in the West of England for over 30 years. He has been teaching mindfulness to patients and staff for most of that time. Fifteen years ago, his own profound experience of 'letting go' radically changed the way he lives and works. Since then, a non-dual perspective has informed his mindfulness teaching and practice, his work as a psychotherapist, his relationships and his overall approach to life.

He lives with his New Zealand born wife and Shetland sheep dog. Their two daughters and four grandchildren live nearby.

Books by the Author

Sitting in the Stillness

Mantra books, John Hunt Publishing, 2020

ISBN 978-1-78904-266-5

What if there is, fundamentally, nothing to change or fix in ourselves?

Sitting in the Stillness is a collection of stories from the therapy room. Each one invites the reader to go beyond these personal accounts to the universal, beyond the agitations of the mind to an infinite stillness of being. The stories include examples from group therapy, mindfulness groups, family and couples therapy and demonstrate our fundamental inter-connectedness.

No one Playing

Mantra books, John Hunt Publishing, 2022

ISBN 978-1-78904-781-3

Intention is in tension – learning to take the stress out of performance. *No one Playing* is a story about a strange encounter on the golf course with someone who, on the face of it, knows nothing about golf but who ends up teaching the author about the inner game and questioning his approach to golf and to life itself.

The book is not just about golf or sport, nor about improvement or progress or how to do something. If anything, it points to a way of living effortlessly that is free and harmonious, that is, to the essence of mindfulness and non-duality.

Each of the nineteen chapters contains a lesson which the author palpably resists for the first few holes. But gradually he comes to realise the profound truth in the teachings of the stranger and begins to understand the radical perspective of no one playing.

MANTRA
BOOKS

EASTERN RELIGION & PHILOSOPHY

We publish books on Eastern religions and philosophies. Books
that aim to inform and explore the various traditions that began in
the East and have migrated West.
If you have enjoyed this book, why not tell other readers by
posting a review on your preferred book site.

The Way of Nothing
Nothing in the Way
Paramananda Ishaya
A fresh and light-hearted exploration of the amazing reality of
nothingness.
Paperback: 978-1-78279-307-6 ebook: 978-1-78099-840-4

Readers of ebooks can buy or view any of these bestsellers by
clicking on the live link in the title. Most titles are published in
paperback and as an ebook. Paperbacks are available in traditional
bookshops. Both print and ebook formats are available online.

Find more titles and sign up to our readers' newsletter at
http://www.johnhuntpublishing.com/mind-body-spirit.
Follow us on Facebook at https://www.facebook.com/OBooks
and Twitter at https://twitter.com/obooks.